REH ★ PRO LESSONS

JAZZ IMPROVISATION
for Guitar

by Les Wise

PLAYBACK+
Speed • Pitch • Balance • Loop

To access audio visit:
www.halleonard.com/mylibrary

7543-9825-9259-4312

ISBN 978-0-634-03356-8

HAL•LEONARD®

7777 W. BLUEMOUND RD. P.O. BOX 13819 MILWAUKEE, WI 53213

Visit Hal Leonard Online at
www.halleonard.com

About the Author

In 1978, Les Wise was selected to join the staff at the Guitar Institute of Technology (G.I.T.) in Hollywood, California. Previously, he taught jazz guitar at Loyola University in New Orleans, Louisiana. Les has played with such stars as Lou Rawls, Jack Jones, Peggy Lee, Nancy Wilson, and Tony Bennett. His playing has been featured on countless albums, jingles, and commercials. Besides teaching at the G.I.T. and recording, Les heads his own quartet and is authoring several guitar instructional books.

Note from the Author

I hope this book will provide you with a fresh outlook on the subject of improvisation. You should also be listening to other instruments and learning from as many sources as you can. Remember that improvising also means taking chances, experimenting, and really listening to what you play. Without these elements, improvised music is robbed of its essential drama and spontaneity.

Introduction

There have been many books written on the subject of jazz improvisation. Many of these books simply contain an abundance of scales to be used when soloing. While the learning of scales is certainly essential, I feel the more important lesson lies in learning to make actual music with the scales you know. The overall purpose of "Jazz Improvisation for Guitar" is to equip the guitarist with the necessary tools to make the transition from playing disjointed scales and arpeggios to playing melodic solos that maintain continuity and interest for the listener.

Contents

Tension and Resolution

One of the keys to improvisation is the control of consonance (resolution) and dissonance (tension). Without this fundamental concept, solos will many times sound as though they are "going nowhere." To state it very simply: dissonance (tension) should be followed by consonance (resolution).

What we are going to concentrate on in this book is how to create and control tension as it applies to single-note soloing.

Scale Harmonization

Scale harmonization is accomplished by the vertical stacking of successive intervals in thirds. The diagram below shows a harmonized C major scale. You should get accustomed to using Roman numeral notation and realize that, although the letter names will change, the chord forms will remain the same for any harmonized major scale.

HARMONIZED C MAJOR SCALE

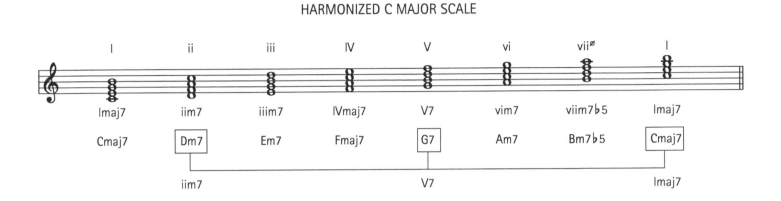

Notice that it is from major scale harmonization that we derive the major ii–V–I progression. Be sure you understand this, as it is essential for jazz improvisation. Here is what a typical ii–V–I progression in C major might look like:

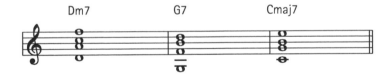

Natural and Altered Tension

Since G7 is the V chord in the key of C, the C major scale not only gives us the chordal tones of G7 (G, B, D, and F), but also extension tones 9, 11, and 13 (A, C, and E). We will call these *natural tension tones.* The natural tension tones do *not* change the function of the chord; they only add flavor.

NATURAL TENSION: (for G7, G9, G11, or G13)

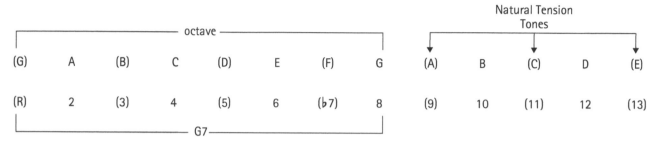

ALTERED TENSION: (for G+7, G7♭5, G9♭5, G13♭9, etc.)

When we talk about altered tension tones, we are referring to the alteration (flatting or sharping) of the 5th and/or 9th degrees of the dominant chord. It implies movement and therefore is used over the functioning (or moving) dominant 7th chord.

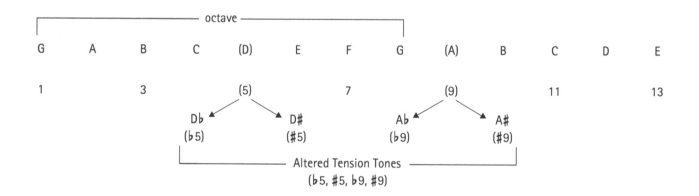

The Dominant 7th Chord

The dominant 7th chord can only act in two different ways. It can either be non-functioning or functioning.

NON-FUNCTIONING

This is when the dominant 7th chord is static or lasts for more than one measure. Static dominant 7th chords are often found in a vamp progression. When the dominant 7th chord is non-functioning, use natural tension.

VAMP PROGRESSION

FUNCTIONING

This is when the dominant 7th chord is moving or resolving to the following chord. It can be the V chord of a major, minor, or dominant chord. For example: G7 to C, G7 to Cm7, or G7 to C7.

When the dominant 7th chord is functioning, use altered tension. This creates a tension-and-release effect, leading the listener to the next point of rest in the solo.

Major Scale Patterns

These are three very common major scale patterns. Be sure that you are familiar with them, as we are going to be using them to illustrate our musical examples.

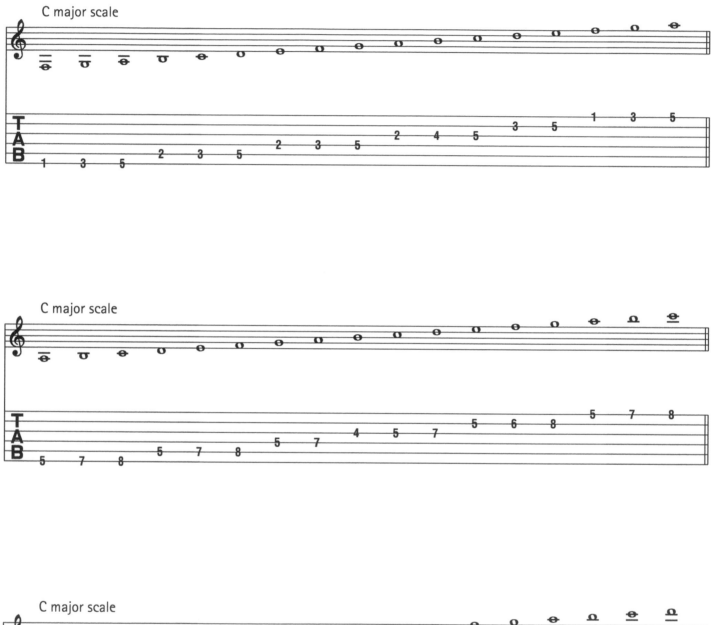

Tension and Resolution with Major Scales

The following exmples only make use of notes found in the C major scale.

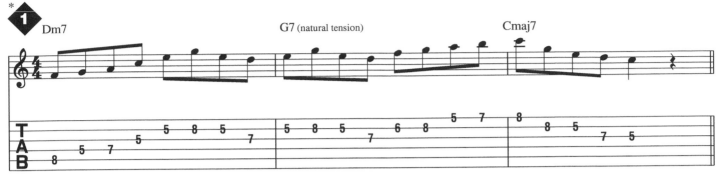

*example 1 is found on track 1 following the introduction music.

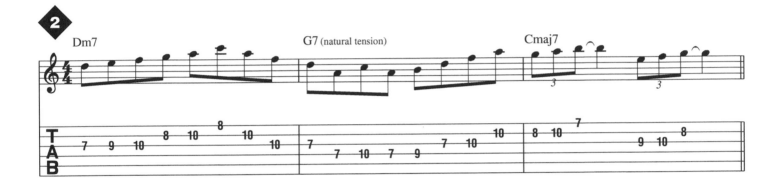

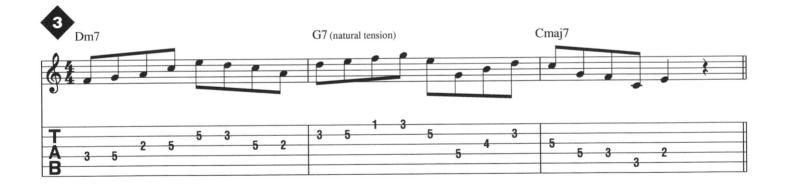

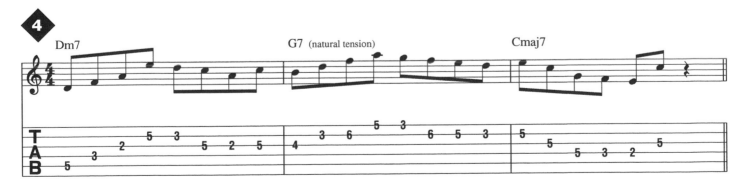

Finding Functioning Dominant 7th Chords

The secret of great players is their skill in leading the listener from one point in the solo to the next. We can accomplish this by locating the functioning dominant 7th chords (V of the next chord) and controlling the tension on it. Our first step is to be able to spot this functioning dominant 7th chord. Here is a standard chord progression showing this V–I relationship. You will notice that sometimes the V chord is part of a ii–V–I progression, and sometimes it's just a V chord all by itself.

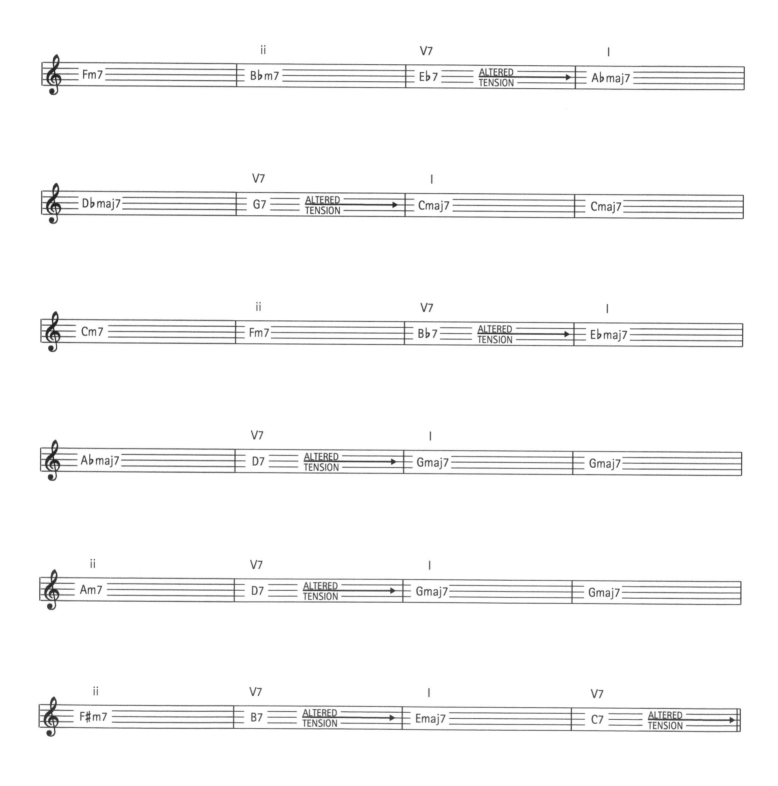

Altered Tension with the Major Scale

Creating altered tension can be simple if we relate it to something basic. We know that if we play the major scale from which the dominant 7th chord is built, we can only get natural tension tones. But by playing a major scale over the dominant 7th chord that is not diatonic to the dominant 7th chord's key center, we can automatically create altered tension tones.

RULE: Play a major scale one half-step higher than the root of the dominant 7th chord (i.e. for G7, play A♭ major scale).

					Natural Tension Tones		
G7 chord =	G	B	D	F	A	C	E
intervals =	1	3	5	♭7	9	11	13

A♭ major scale =	A♭	B♭	C	D♭	E♭	F	G	A♭
against G7 chord =	♭9	♯9	11	♭5	♯5	♭7	R	♭9

Notice how this automatically produces all the altered tension tones (♭9, ♯9, ♭5, ♯5).

G7 chord

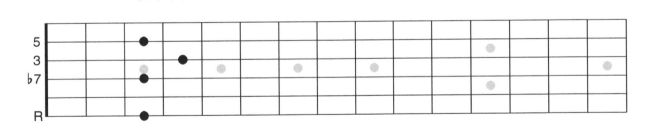

A♭ major scale

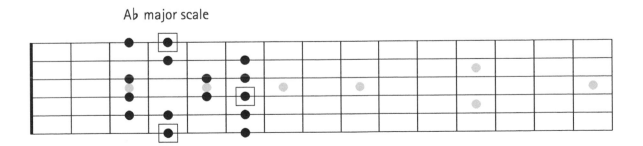

Altered Tension with the Major Arpeggio

RULE: Play the major arpeggio one half-step higher than the root of the dominant 7th chord (i.e. for G7 chord, play A♭maj9 arpeggio).

					Natural Tension Tones		
G7 chord =	G	B	D	F	A	C	E
	1	3	5	♭7	9	11	13

A♭maj9 arpeggio =	A♭	C	E♭	G	B♭
against G7 chord =	♭9	11	#5	R	#9

Notice how this automatically produces the following altered tension tones: ♭9, #5, and #9.

G7 chord

A♭maj9 arpeggio

R 3 5 7 R 3 5 7 9

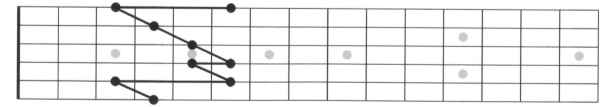

Altered Tension in the ii–V–I Progression

Since most tunes are comprised of ii–V–I progressions (Dm7–G7–C, Cm7–F7–B♭, Am7–D7–G, Em7–A7–D, etc.) in varying lengths, it is essential that we build a repertoire of creative and melodic phrases to play over this progression. One way to accomplish this is by using major scales. By simply knowing the major scale (and where to play it), we can create our tension-and-release effect, making the major scale a very powerful tool in improvising.

In the musical examples ahead, you will notice the use of the Fmaj7 chord shape over the Dm7 chord. We can do this because the IVmaj7 chord is a very common chord substitute for the iim7 chord (Fmaj7 = Dm9). The following analysis should clarify this.

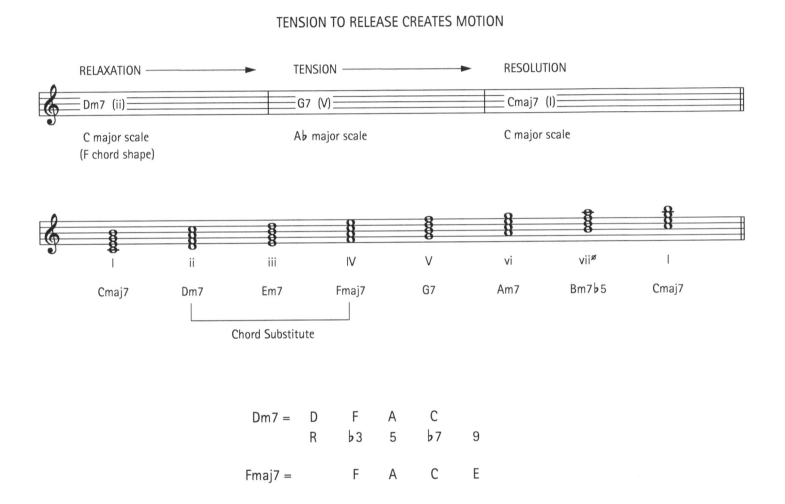

Notice that when we play the notes of the Fmaj7 (IV) chord over the Dm7 (ii) chord, we exchange the root (D) for the 9th (E). This gives us the sound of Dm9.

Playing the Examples from Chord Forms

Although the examples may be played in various positions (and should be), they are graphically displayed here using these three common chord forms as one possibility. You should experiment with other chord forms to broaden your knowledge of the guitar fretboard.

Dm7
Fmaj7 chord form
(C major scale)

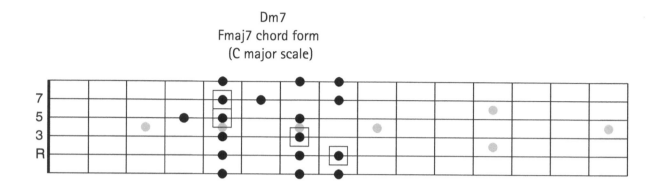

G7
A♭maj7 chord form
(A♭ major scale)

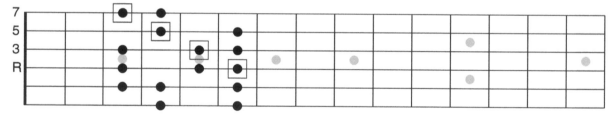

Cmaj7
Cmaj7 chord form
(C major scale)

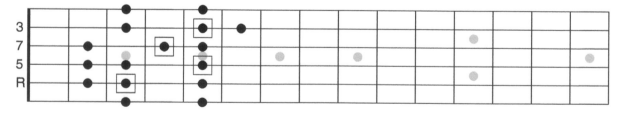

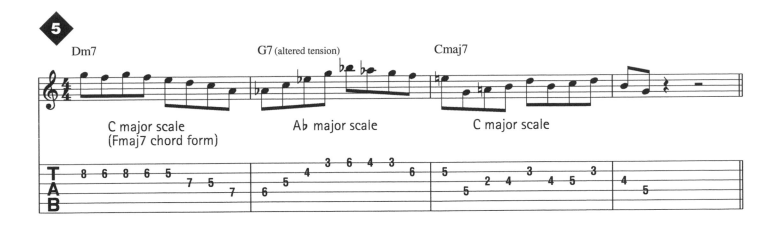

Although the major scale examples we graphically displayed utilize various chord forms, you should also play them using just one chord form and moving it to the appropriate place. This offers simplicity in thinking, as you can easily repeat one lick or idea through the entire progression. Use the first major 7 chord form for the ii chord, then simply move the hand up the neck a minor 3rd (3 frets) for the V7 chord. Finally, move up a major 3rd (4 frets) higher to accommodate the I chord. You can see that with all the ii-V-I progressions in tunes, this is a powerful tool.

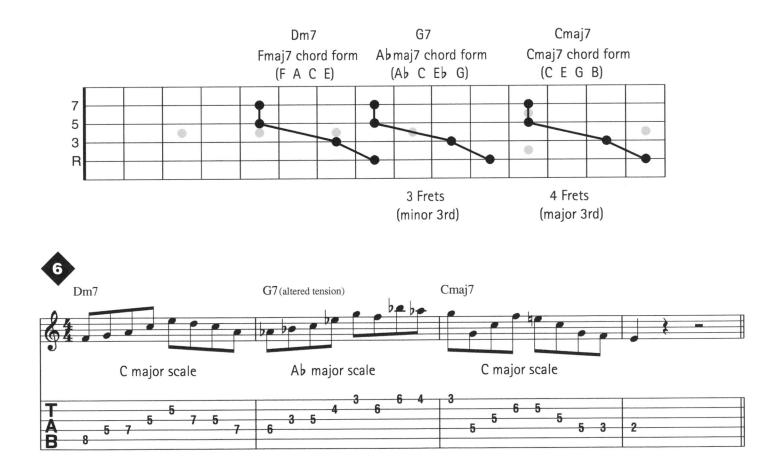

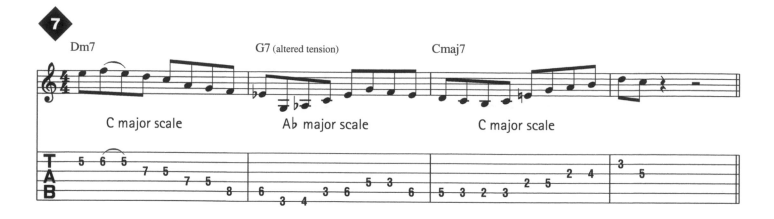

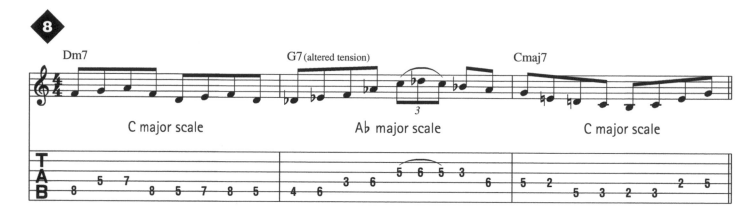

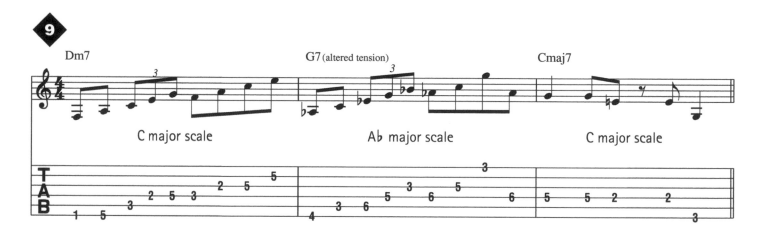

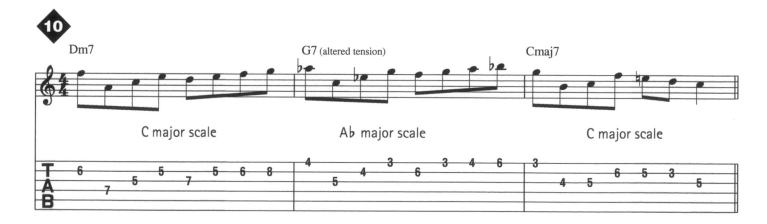

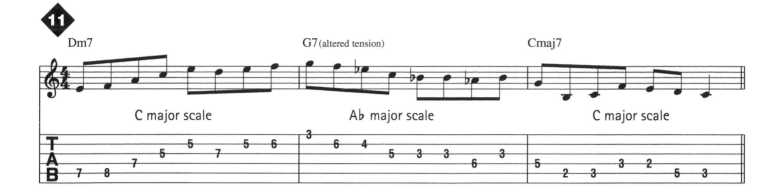

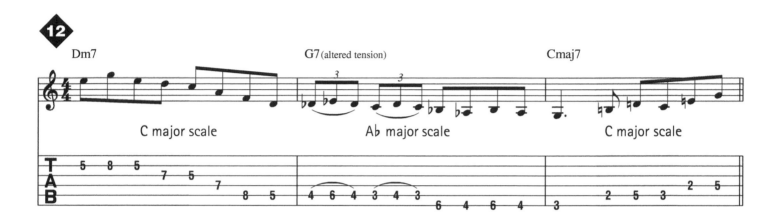

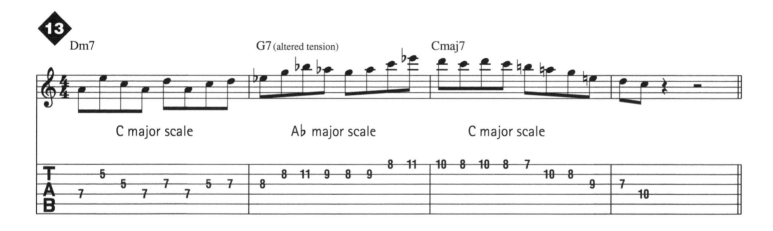

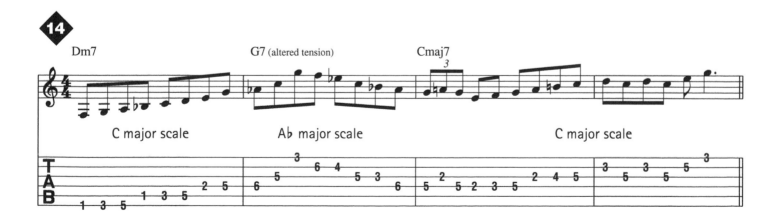

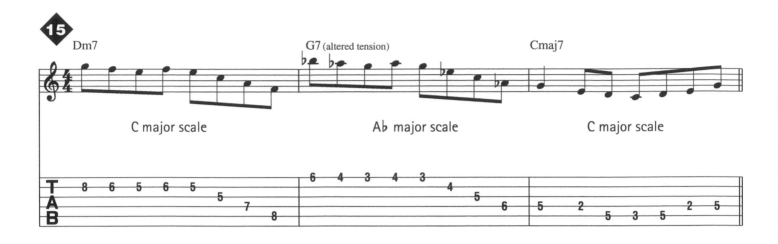

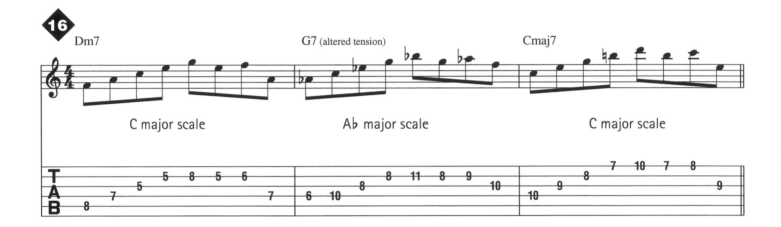

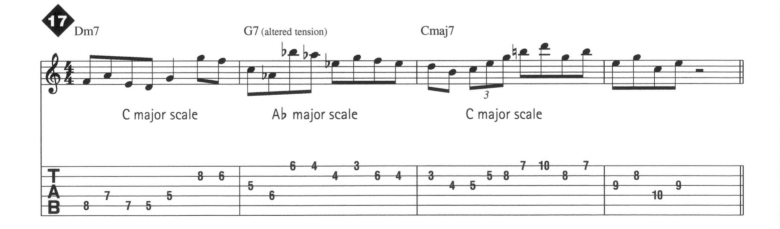

The Jazz or "Real" Melodic Minor Scale

The jazz or "real" melodic minor scale is simply a major scale with a lowered 3rd degree. Notice how this scale gives us a combined major and minor effect.

A♭ major scale:	A♭	B♭	C	D♭	E♭	F	G	A♭
	1	2	3	4	5	6	7	1

By lowering the 3rd of the A♭ major scale, this scale becomes an A♭ jazz minor scale.

HARMONIZED A♭ JAZZ MINOR SCALE

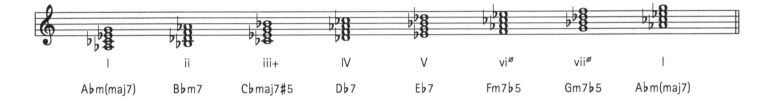

I	ii	iii+	IV	V	vi°	vii°	I
A♭m(maj7)	B♭m7	C♭maj7♯5	D♭7	E♭7	Fm7♭5	Gm7♭5	A♭m(maj7)

RULE: Play a jazz melodic minor scale one half-step higher than the root of the dominant 7th chord (i.e. for G7, play A♭ melodic minor scale).

A♭ jazz minor =	A♭	B♭	C♭	D♭	E♭	F	G	A♭
against G7 chord =	♭9	♯9	3	♭5	♯5	♭7	R	♭9

Because this scale contains a B (C♭) note (the 3rd of G7), it gives us a strong G7 chordal sound.

Starting on the root of the jazz minor scale, the arpeggio we derive is an A♭m(maj7) arpeggio. Remember, this is simply an A♭maj7 or 9 arpeggio with a lowered 3rd degree.

A♭m(maj7) arpeggio =	A♭	C♭	E♭	G
against G7 chord =	♭9	3	♯5	R

Melodic Minor Scale and Arpeggio Forms

Ab melodic minor scale

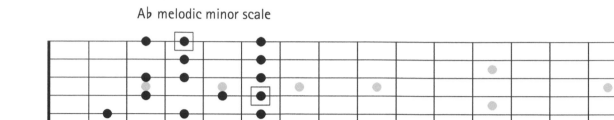

Abm(maj7) arpeggio

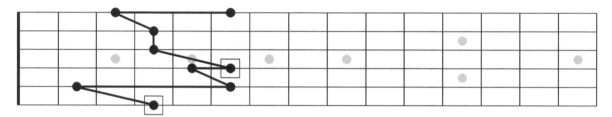

Ab melodic minor scale

Abm(maj7) arpeggio

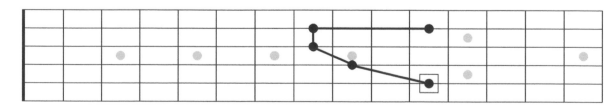

Tension and Resolution with Jazz Minor

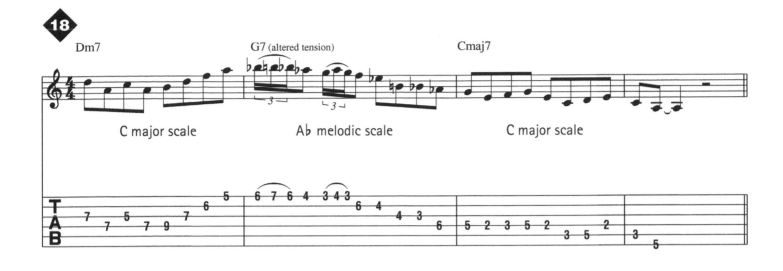

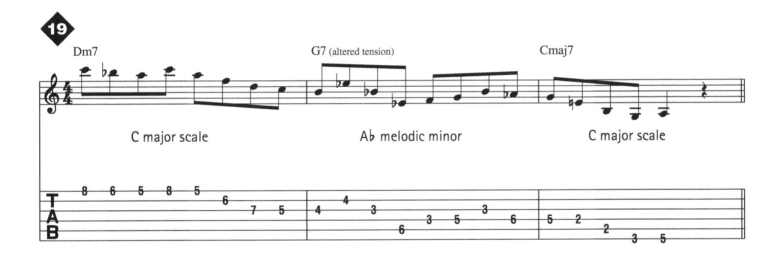

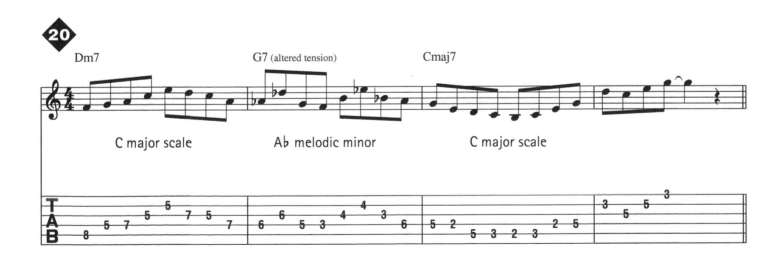

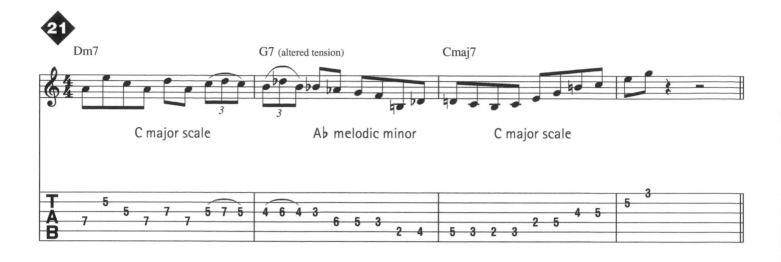

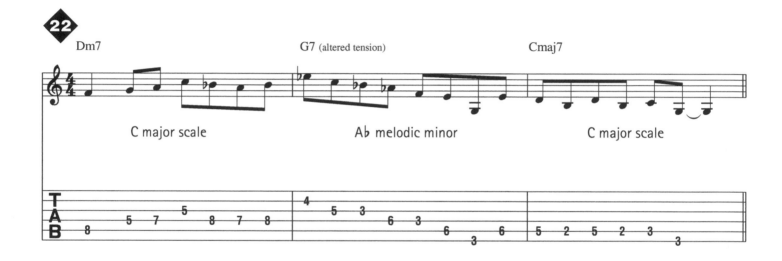

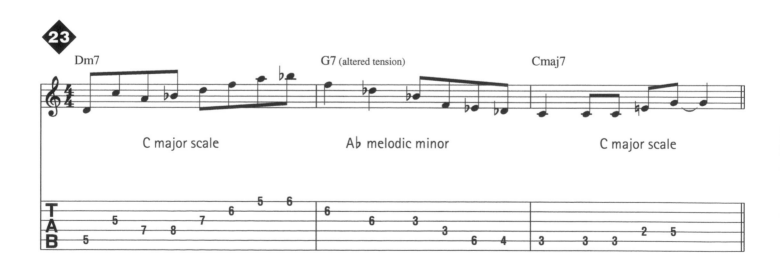

The Harmonic Minor Scale

Our last scale will be the harmonic minor. We will make use of the A and C harmonic minor scales. The harmonic minor scale is simply a major scale with lowered 3rd and 6th degrees. Several arpeggios from the A and C harmonic minor scales create interesting tension. Notice the A harmonic minor offers natural tension tones using the ii⌀, iv, and VI arpeggios and altered tension using the III+, V, and vii° arpeggios. The C harmonic minor offers natural tension using the V arpeggio, while the other arpeggios offer altered tension tones.

HARMONIZED A HARMONIC MINOR SCALE

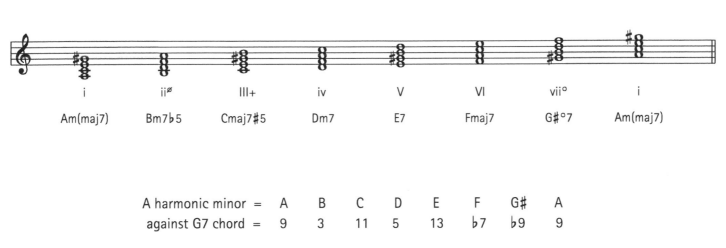

	A harmonic minor =	A	B	C	D	E	F	G#	A
	against G7 chord =	9	3	11	5	13	♭7	♭9	9

HARMONIZED C HARMONIC MINOR SCALE

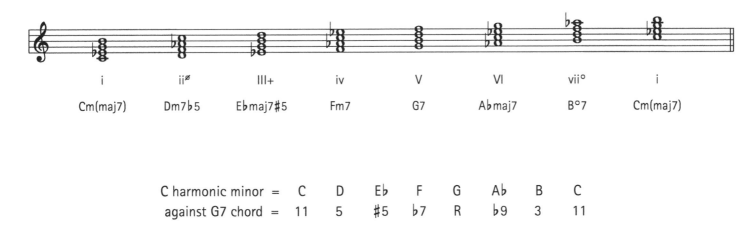

	C harmonic minor =	C	D	E♭	F	G	A♭	B	C
	against G7 chord =	11	5	#5	♭7	R	♭9	3	11

Harmonic Minor Scale Forms

A harmonic minor scale

A harmonic minor scale

C harmonic minor scale

C harmonic minor scale

Tension and Resolution with Harmonic Minor

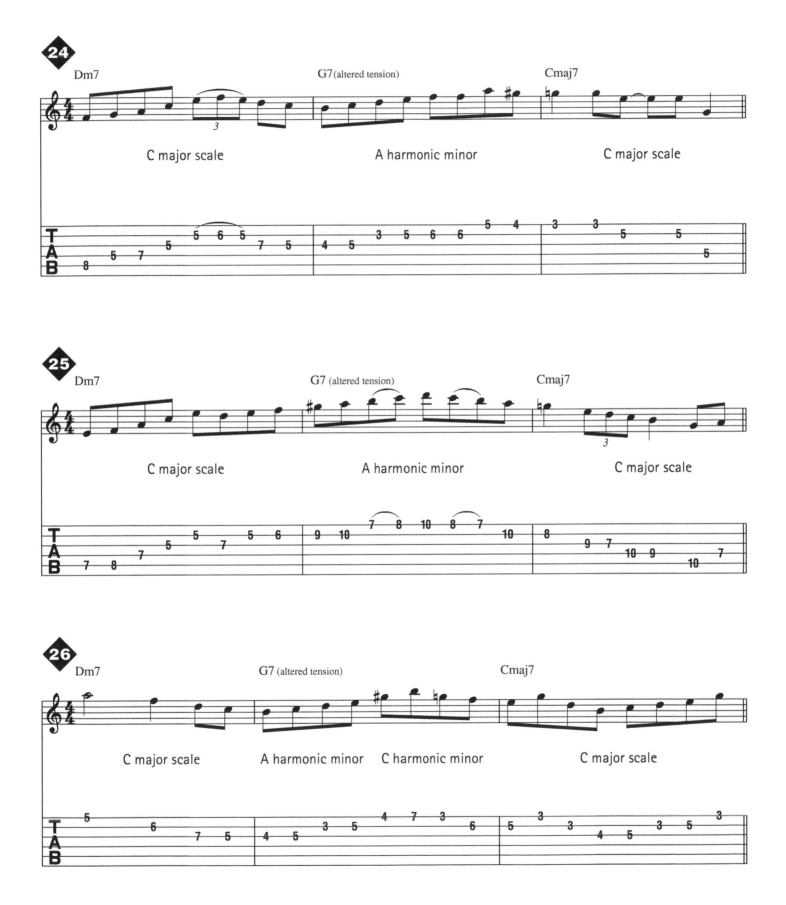

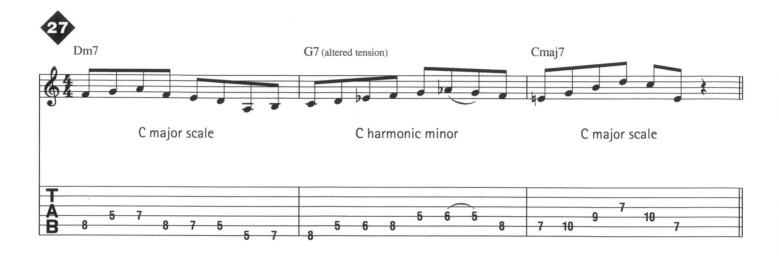

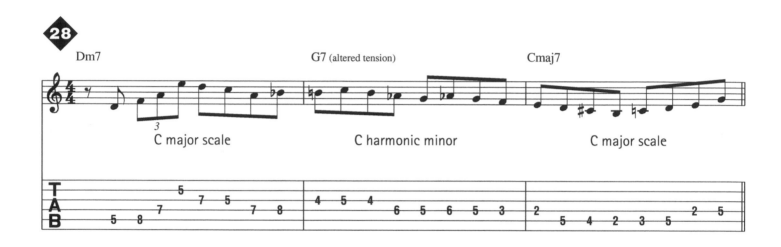

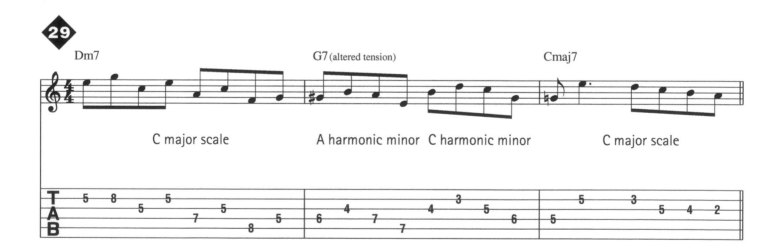

The Minor ii⌀–V–i Progression

We will now learn how to play over the minor ii⌀–V–i progression (Bm7♭5–E7♭9–Am7, Gm7♭5–C7♭9–Fm7 etc.). Let's first look at where the minor ii⌀–V comes from.

A HARMONIC MINOR SCALE (HARMONIZED)

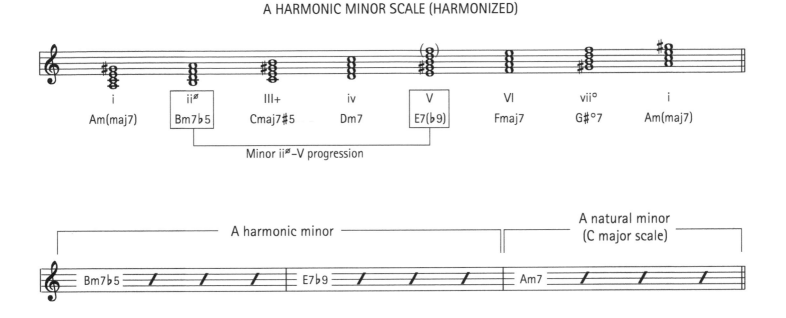

A close examination of the major and minor ii–V–I progressions will reveal some interesting facts.

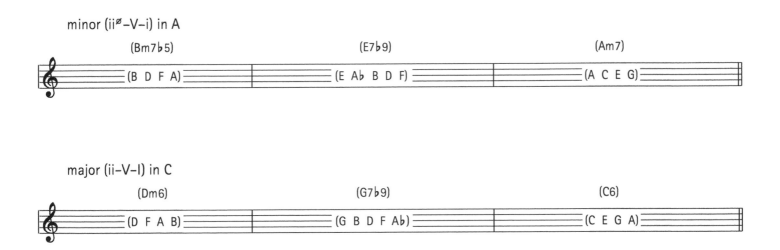

Notice that the notes in the two progressions are almost the same. Because of this relationship, an interesting substitution possibility arises. Whenever you see a minor ii⌀–V–vi progression, you can simply play a major ii–V–I progression starting a minor 3rd (3 frets) above the root of the ii⌀ chord.

Minor ii∅–V–i Examples

30

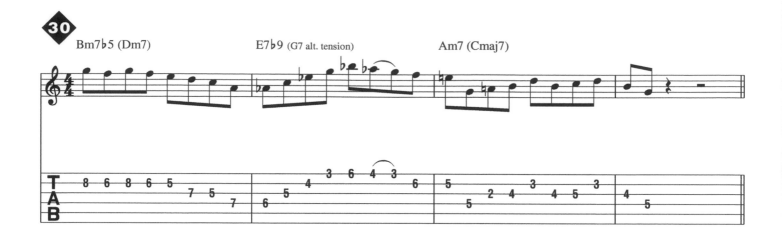

31

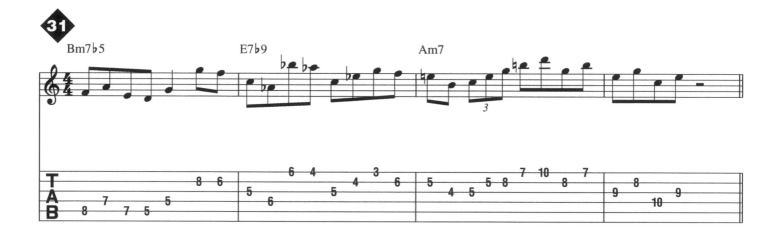

32

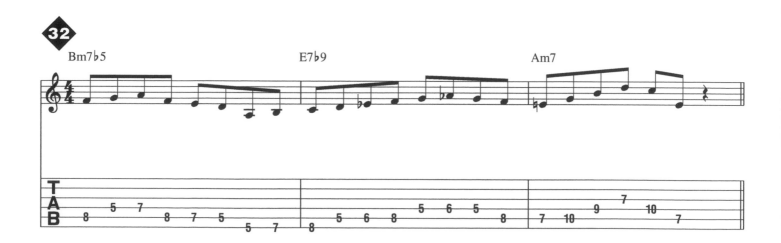

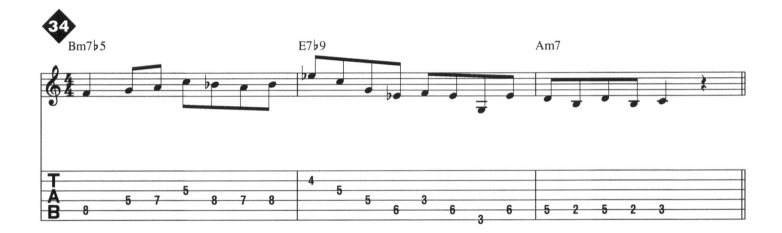

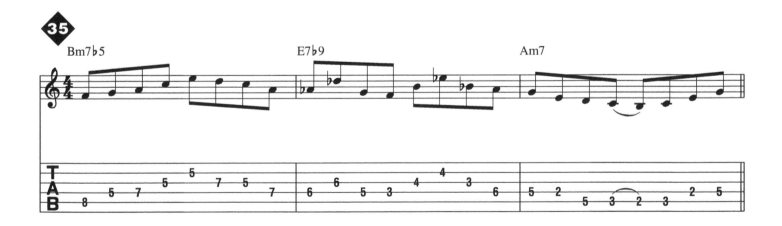

Jazz Guitar Thinking

In jazz soloing, the major and minor scales account for a large percentage of modern improvisation. The trick is to learn to shift the scales we know to fit whatever chord we encounter. This cuts down on the amount of information we have to think about, making intuitive playing easier to reach!

There are only three types of sounds in improvising.

I	II	III
MAJOR	MINOR	DOMINANT
C	Cm	C7, C9, C11
C6	Cm6	C13
Cmaj7	Cm7	C+7
Cmaj9	Cm9	C7♭5
	Cm7♭5	C7♯9
		C7♭9 (B°dim)
		etc.

All chords and scales fall into one of the three columns.

THE DOMINANT 7TH CHORD: This chord is very important. Because of the amount of tension we can apply, much of our motion in our solos comes from this chord. We learned that dominant 7th chords act in two ways: non-functioning (static) and functioning (moving). Now in order to develop continuity in our solos, we must learn to find all functioning dominant 7th chords. By increasing the tension on this chord, we lead the listener through the solo.

With regards to the altered tension (♯5, ♭5, ♯9, ♭9), you can use any of the scales I've given you for any altered chord (G7♭5, G7♯5, G7♯9, G7♭9 etc.) you encounter. You don't have to play a specific scale to fit the altered note. When you see a dominant chord with one alteration, simply apply the scale substitution principles we are learning and don't worry about any additional alterations that may occur.

Resolution in Soloing

When you are soloing over a chord that leads to the next chord, you must resolve properly. This means you must choose a note of the new chord that will lead the listener smoothly from the previous chord. You should strive to move only a half step (either lower or higher) to reach a chord tone of the next chord. This makes for an uninterrupted line and a smooth resolution. Certain chord tones tend to be stronger points of resolution than others. The chart below will illustrate this.

TWO CHORDS PER BAR

Soloists are often troubled when encountering rapid chord changes. In most instances, chords that change every two beats will indicate a sequence of ii–V progressions. In this case, the solution is simple. When two chords in the same measure are from the same key, simply play the scale that both chords are inherent to. For example, since Dm7 and G7 are both in the key of C, you can treat them both as C major. Another possibility would be to simply play the entire measure just thinking of the first chord.

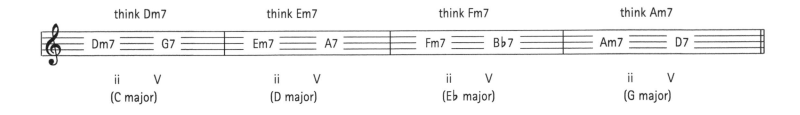

Putting It All Together

These are the chord changes of a popular tune utilizing most of the principles discussed in this book.